Reflections
OF
NEW ENGLAND

Reflections OF NEW ENGLAND

Ellen Lesser

GALLERY BOOKS

Text
Ellen Lesser

Design
Roger Hyde

Photography
Amstock
Black Star
New England Photo Library

Photo Editor
Annette Lerner

Project Director
Sandra Still

This edition published by
Gallery Books, an imprint of
W.H. Smith Publishers, Inc.,
112 Madison Avenue,
New York 10016.
Color separations by Advance Laser
Graphic Arts, Hong Kong.
Printed and bound in Italy.
ISBN 0 83176 361 2

Gallery Books are available for bulk
purchase for sales promotions and
premium use. For details write or
telephone the Manager of Special Sales,
W.H. Smith Publishers, Inc.,
112 Madison Avenue, New York,
New York 10016 (212) 532-6600

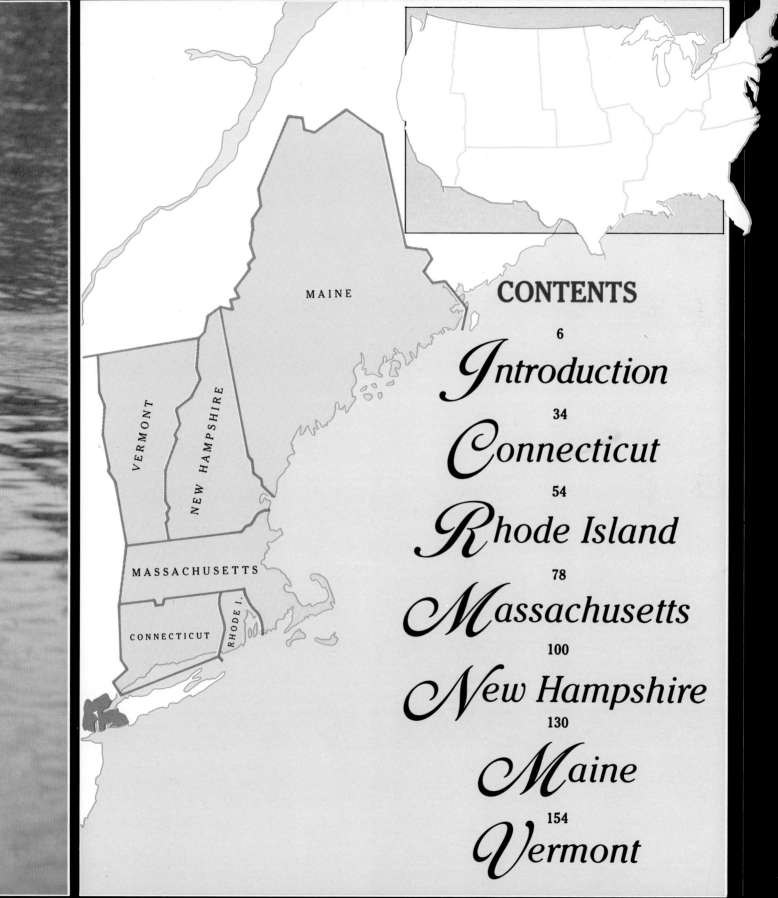

MAINE

VERMONT

NEW HAMPSHIRE

MASSACHUSETTS

CONNECTICUT

RHODE I.

CONTENTS

Above: *nine 'seafensibles,' folk art on a Rockport roof.*
Right: *glorious fall trees and tidy wooden houses find their reflection in Parlin Pond in west Maine.*

Introduction

To speak the words New England *is to conjure a store of magical images. Maybe what springs to mind first is a classic red clapboard farmhouse with its parade of weathered barns and silos and sheds snaking across a green hillside, leaning and sagging with the hill's contours until the buildings themselves become almost a part of the landscape. Or it might be a white frame, steepled church, severe yet elegant in its simplicity as it beckons across a pristine village common. There's the welcoming portal of an old wooden covered bridge crossing a summer-lazy stream, or a lone lighthouse's beacon cutting through fog from a rocky promontory above the crashing Atlantic.*

For some, the mention of New England summons a picture of a back road at the tail end of winter, lined with stately sugar maples decked out in the rough jewels of battered steel sap buckets; for others, a vision of a sunbaked lobsterman's shack, walls lively with their mosaic of buoys and yard littered with lobster traps, their wooden slats silvered by the briny elements.

For everyone who thinks *New England* and imagines a country lane turned dazzling with autumn foliage, there's someone else seeing a trail through pines slumped gracefully beneath the first heavy snowfall. For every fisherman longing for misty early mornings on a remote northern lake, there's a sailor dreaming of sunset in a sheltering harbor. Every gulp of bracing mountain air has a corresponding whiff of salt breeze; for every tract of seemingly undisturbed wilderness there's a city, crowded with people and history.

Among all the regions of the United States, New England is by far the smallest. All six of its states combined take up less than 67,000 square miles – not even half of Montana, a mere quarter of Texas, eleven percent of Alaska. From Boston, often considered New England's hub, you can hop into a car and be in any of

Above: *a Bethel home, Maine.*

Merrimack. In Manchester, a small mill built on the Amoskeag Falls in 1805 grew into the mammoth Amoskeag Manufacturing Company, whose red brick mill buildings still stretch for a mile downstream along the river's east bank. By the turn of the century, Amoskeag claimed to be the world's largest textile mill, producing four million yards of cloth a week and employing seventeen thousand people. But even its gargantuan scale couldn't insulate the mill from the economic forces that brought down New England's textile business as a whole. In 1936, A.M.C. filed for bankruptcy.

Before the mass exodus from the upcountry farms, New Hampshire also had its share in rural New England's flowering. Along the western edge of the state, in the Upper Connecticut River Valley, lie the fertile meadows and peaceful villages that epitomize the New England farmscape. The valley has its cultural center in Hanover, where Dartmouth's common, flanked by white frame halls with their trademark green shutters and aged copper roofs, defines the image of collegiate New England as surely as Harvard's red brick. It was in arguing a case about Dartmouth's legal status before the Supreme Court in

Above: *a summer tour boat on Lake Winnipesaukee.*

Right: *a pumpkin-headed scarecrow, Londonderry.*

Above: *countryside near Bradford, east of Concord.*

Left: *beside the Ashuelot River, southern New Hampshire.*

1818 that the school's most famous alumnus, Daniel Webster, remarked: "It is . . . a small college, and yet there are those who love it."

It wasn't only the graceful landscape or intellectual sophistication of New Hampshire's Upper Valley that drew sculptor Augustus Saint-Gaudens in the 1880s. The artist known as America's Michelangelo was planning a statue of Lincoln. The owner of a defunct inn in Cornish lured him with the promise of the many "Lincoln-shaped" men among the Yankee populace. Saint-Gaudens, creator of heroic works such as the Shaw Memorial on Boston Common, is credited with redefining American public sculpture. He also redefined the hill town of Cornish, turning the crumbling Federal tavern into a neoclassical country

estate, complete with columned porch, formal gardens, and sculpture studios. In the process, he attracted the group of fellow artists who would come to be known as the Cornish Colony. Among those who followed Saint-Gaudens to the New Hampshire hills was popular illustrator and painter, Maxfield Parrish. Even a quick glimpse at the Cornish countryside in the right light makes Parrish's intense signature blues seem a good deal less fantastical.

If central New Hampshire's western corridor is shaped by the Connecticut Valley, its eastern section is defined by its lakes. In all, New Hampshire boasts a total of thirteen hundred lakes and ponds, but the central Lake District is studded with an unusual concentration, the jewel in the crown being Lake

Above: *fly-fishing at Saco Lake near Crawford Notch in the White Mountains.*

Above: *a steam train puffs downhill on the Mount Washington Cog Railway.*

Left: *soft gold fall foliage graces a misty pond in Laconia.*

Winnipesaukee. The Indian word that gives New England's second largest lake its name has been variously translated as "Beautiful Water in a High Place" and "Smile of the Great Spirit." Either description fits the magnificent Winnipesaukee, with its 183 miles of shoreline, 274 islands, and numerous bays, which have brought vacationers to resort towns like Wolfeboro and Laconia since the eighteenth century.

Perhaps more than any other New England state, New Hampshire possesses a split personality. The populous, heavily developed southern tier is dismissed by some as a suburb of Boston. If central New Hampshire doesn't provide enough of a contrast, one need only move farther north. Crossing into the

White Mountain National Forest will erase any doubt that New Hampshire has its share of protected wilderness. Robert Frost once opined, "The only fault I find with New Hampshire is that her mountains aren't quite high enough." The Whites may be no match for the great western chains when it comes to size, but they offer the most rugged landscape their side of the Rockies. New Hampshire's mountains are only the worn-down remnants of an ancient range, but erosion didn't give them the gentler, rounded look of the Greens in Vermont. The igneous activity that gave birth to the Whites leaves its mark in the drama of the peaks' jagged skyline.

Of the White Mountains' three ranges, the most towering is the Presidential, with eighty-six peaks

ranging from 5,380 to 6,288 feet above sea level. The Presidentials' giant is Mt. Washington. From the summit, on exceptionally clear days, it's possible to see seventy-five miles to the ocean. The summit's meteorological station does nothing to dispute Mt. Washington's claim to having the country's worst weather. The highest wind velocity ever recorded – 231 miles per hour – was clocked at the station during a 1934 storm. Winter readings of two hundred m.p.h. aren't unusual; neither are snow and sub-freezing temperatures during the summertime. Climbing a mountain has often been likened to traveling north, and the comparison certainly holds for Washington. The mountain's upper elevations present a classic example of what happens to vegetation when you enter the Alpine zone.

The ascent begins in familiar northern hardwood forest, but gradually the maples and birch disappear, making way for an almost solid stand of spruce and fir. As you continue to climb, the boreal conifers grow progressively shorter and more gnarled in the face of fierce winds, until they cease to be trees at all, but dense, horizontal mats called Krummholz, German for "crooked wood." Then, suddenly, even the twisted mats disappear, and you're over the treeline. The

Above: trees alive with the color for which southern New Hampshire is famous.

Facing page: Franconia Ridge viewed from the Hi-Cannon Trail in the White Mountains.

Alpine summits may appear lifeless – practically lunar – when viewed from below, but above the treeline vegetation persists, filling every available crevice. The rocks support various lichens, sedges, and mosses, and over a hundred species of flowering plants, many of which also grow in northern Canada's Arctic tundra. The flowers peak in the Presidentials during the last week in June, when bunches of white, yellow, and bright pink blooms burst forth from the cracks in the stone, turning the solemn, upper slopes into a dazzling rock garden.

Hiking up Mt. Washington poses a serious challenge, but the trip along the winding, eight-mile auto route is intimidating in its own right. As you emerge from the conifer forest into the Krummholz, and the breathtaking views start opening up, it can seem as if the already-too-narrow road were dropping away from beneath you. However mild it was when you set out from the base, chances are good you'll have a bitter dash from your car to the summit lodge entrance. The drive down in low gear – alternately

Facing page: *steam and snow on the eleven-mile-long Conway Scenic Railroad.*

Above: *Mount Washington Hotel in White Mountain National Forest.*

pumping the brakes and stopping to cool them – may be the worst trial of all. The sticker claiming, "This Car Climbed Mt. Washington," will be well-earned, but if you ever plan to resell the vehicle, you'll probably want to keep the boast off your bumper. Many view-seekers still choose to ride the Cog Railway, whose steam-powered cars have been chugging up and down their steeply-graded tracks for well over a century.

On the glacial plain at Mt. Washington's base, the inns of Bretton Woods have welcomed sportsmen, vacationers, and artists from as early as 1800. In 1944, the palatial turn-of-the-century Mt. Washington Hotel hosted a more political crowd for the Bretton Woods Conference, which established international monetary policies for the post-World-War-II period. It was the area around Franconia, further west, that drew Robert Frost to the mountains. In 1915, when Frost, at age forty, bought an unassuming white clapboard farmhouse perched above Franconia Valley, his work had yet to be published in this country. Before five years of farming and writing were out, he had published three volumes of verse and been awarded the Pulitzer Prize.

The nature trail at the Robert Frost Place features fifteen of Frost's poems, engraved on plaques, to be contemplated along with the scenery. All of Franconia's attractions aren't so gentle, though. There's the spectacular chasm known as Flume Gorge, and Franconia Notch, one of several deep passes that cut through the mountains. Above the Notch, from the top of a cliff, protrudes a series of five granite ledges that looks uncannily like a thoughtful if craggy human face viewed in profile – the Old Man of the Mountain. The region's Indians believed the profile to be the embodiment of the Great Spirit. Daniel Webster, ever the New Hampshire partisan, had this to say about the famous Stone Face: "Men hang out their signs indicative of their respective trades: shoemakers hang out a gigantic shoe; jewelers, a monster watch . . . but up in the mountains of New Hampshire, God Almighty has hung out a sign to show that there He makes men."

The men and women made in New Hampshire are indisputably a particular breed. The epithet of "The Granite State" might refer to the character of the people as much as to the mantle of bedrock. New Hampshire's politics have long been marked by an indelible conservative streak, which has helped keep it the only state in the union without any sales or income tax. When citizens of the Granite State say, "Live free or die," they mean business.

Above: *a downhill skier at the Black Mountain Ski Resort, near Carter Notch, Jackson.*

Right: *a solitary child picking spring wildflowers in a White Mountain meadow.*

Left: *the third hole of the famous Balsams Hotel golf course in Dixville Notch.*

Above: *the John Paul Jones House in Portsmouth.*

Left: *a variation on the post and rail in Center Sandwich.*

114

Right: *the Frost Free Library in Marlborough, near Keene.*

Above: *part of a wall mural in the Warner House, Portsmouth.*

Right: *an interior of the Rose and Thistle, Intervale.*

Left: *a Sugar Hill church, as white as snow all year round.*

Above: *a huge snow sculpture on the Green at Dartmouth College, Hanover.*

Right: *inspirational words on a blackboard in a Shaker schoolroom, Canterbury.*

Facing page: *a view of an old cemetery from inside a church at Center Barnstead.*

No one will find a spiritual heaven, until they first create an earthly heaven.

I WILL TRY

Rainbows afloat – hot air balloons glide over Pittsfield, northeast of Concord.

Above: *dam water glittering as winter grips Chocorua, a village in the White Mountains.*

Left: *the cupola of elegant and well-preserved Warner House, built in Portsmouth in 1716.*

Right: *a waterfall alongside the Falling Waters Trail in White Mountain National Forest.*

Above: *Old Glory hangs outside a Newbury general store.*

Below: *a model Indian outside a Moultonborough store.*

Right: *mist swirls near resting hikers on Mount Lafayette.*

124

Above: *a house preserved by the Strawberry Banke renewal project in Portsmouth.*

Facing page top: *peas in a pod – row house chimneys in the mill district of Manchester.*

Right: *full moon behind the lighthouse at Newcastle.*

Facing page bottom: *the Flume Covered Bridge in Franconia.*

Above: *a winter sleigh ride in Canterbury, north of Concord.*

Above: *storm clouds gathering over Hanover pastureland.*

Left: *the traditional method of maple sugaring in spring.*

A common loon, a bird that winters in New Hampshire.

Above: *sunrise along the rocky, very romantic coast of Maine.*
Right: *a homeward-bound dinghy in Vinalhaven harbor.*

*M*aine

When sixteenth-century explorers reconnoitered the coast of
*Maine, they were hunting for a land they called Norumbega, a country of untold
riches like the El Dorado Cortes was seeking in Mexico. Through much of that
century, Europe's mapmakers fixed the fabled Paradise on the Penobscot River.
In Mexico, the European adventurers found their grail in the Aztec empire, with
its legendary stores of gold; up north, Norumbega was only a fantasy. The myth
was laid to rest once and for all when Samuel de Champlain surveyed Maine's
coast in 1604. The explorer described the mouth of the Penobscot as "marvelous
to behold." It wasn't paradise, but it was a land of beauty and mystery.*

While Maine's white settlers never found pots of
gold, they did find giant shell heaps, believed to have
been accumulated between one and five thousand
years ago by Indians who traveled to the coast in
summer to reap mighty sea harvests. However, the
archeological evidence of habitation in Maine
stretches back even farther, to early neolithic times.
The superstitious colonists were unnerved by their
discovery of prehistoric graves colored with a brilliant
red ochre. The so-called Red Paint People's tools and
implements have since been collected and studied
extensively, but they guard their secrets; no one
knows where the Red Paints came from, how long
they stayed, and when and why they departed. The
Red Paint People and the shell-heapers were long
gone, but the early settlers found Maine's wooded
shores populated by a branch of the Algonquins who

Above: *fishing floats on
Monhegan Island.*

called themselves Wabanaki, "living at the sunrise," a name that preserved their ancestral memory of a great migration eastward, toward the land of the dawn.

Maine is by far the largest New England state, but even given its size, it flaunts a disproportionately long coastline. From Kittery to Eastport, as the crow flies, it's 250 miles, but between those two points lie twenty-five hundred miles of actual shoreline. And that total doesn't include the shores of Maine's more than three thousand islands. The figure of three thousand – more than on the rest of the eastern seaboard combined – isn't merely a convenient approximation; no precise count of the islands exists. Their number changes too often with the weather, time, and the tides. Suffice it to say that from the tip of Maine's capes, points, necks, and heads, one can spy the windswept and wave-washed multitudes, large and small, studding the water like sequins. One

Above: tools of the trade – lobster pots on the jetty at Friendship.

Facing page bottom: sunrise and solitude on Ferry Beach.

common speculation about the state's name is that it was coined to distinguish the mainland from the islands' vast and various kingdom.

Maine's rugged, accordioned, and island-speckled coast was actually once a mountain range, partially drowned at the end of New England's ice age. For the narrator of Sarah Orne Jewett's quintessential Maine novel, *The Country of the Pointed Firs*, the rocky, mountainous coastline is reminiscent of Greece. Maine's islands share a geological kinship with Greece as well; there, they would be more precisely defined as an archipelago. On both the islands and along the coast, the dramatic interplay of volatile elements might easily give birth to myths about capricious gods similar to those that sprung up in the Aegean.

Above: *Camden harbor as seen from the town park.*

The Maine coast is lined with so many charming resorts and picturesque towns, so many inviting beaches and harbors dotted with lobster boats, it's almost as difficult to account for all of them as it is for the islands. It would be hard to overlook the early settlement of York with its restored village, whose Old Gaol is fortified by the original three-and-a-half-foot-thick fieldstone walls. One should probably mention the Sarah Orne Jewett House in South Berwick, built by Jewett's sea captain grandfather, where, according to local lore, it took three ships' carpenters one hundred days to carve the wainscoting, moldings, and cornices. Going there might mean skipping the Victorian confection in the shipbuilding center-cum-resort of Kennebunk known as the Wedding Cake House, the gift to his young bride of another sea captain, who had to leave port before the couple got

133

to enjoy their real wedding cake.

One shouldn't ignore rocky Cape Elizabeth, thrusting into the Atlantic and guarded by the classic 1790 Portland Head Light, virtually unchanged since George Washington decreed its construction. Then you have to make a stop in Portland as well, to witness the city that wouldn't die. Destroyed twice by Indians, once by the British, once by trade embargo, and later by fire, Portland now thrives as a cultural center, with the refurbished Old Port Exchange a quaint hub of shops and restaurants in the waterfront neighborhood.

Freeport, home to L.L. Bean, is a mecca for both preppie pilgrims and bonafide outdoorspeople. In Bath, the shipyard at the Maine Maritime Museum

continues the tradition of fine hand boatbuilding through its apprenticeship program, perpetuating the craft that produced historic vessels with salty downeast names like Penobscot Bay Pinky, Lighthouse Pea Pod, and Hurricane Island Pulling Boat. The harbors at Rockport and Camden have long been a favorite for yachting enthusiasts. The roughly mid-coast Camden marks the beginning of Maine's more dramatically mountainous coastline. From there, even a summary tour would have to leave the coast for the largest and most famous of Maine's offshore islands – the place Champlain dubbed "*L'isle des monts deserts*," by all accounts the treasure of Maine's rich, long coastline.

Mount Desert Island, a hybrid of mountains and

Above: *winter in Portland, the largest city in Maine.*

Left: *Portland Head Light, the first light built on the east coast after the Revolution.*

Right: *gift shop wares in Bar Harbor, Mount Desert Island.*

shore, is a land of extremes and superlatives. Dividing the island into a pair of roughly equal lobes, the deep, narrow channel of Somes Sound forms the east coast's only fjord. Cadillac Mountain's 1,530-foot summit is the highest point of land along the Atlantic. The craggy Otter Cliffs tower 185 feet over the Gulf of Maine; you have to travel south to Brazil to find taller Atlantic headlands. The waters off Sand Beach, with their summer temperatures frequently as low as fifty degrees, are more hospitable to lobsters and migrating seals than to human swimmers, but the island is also scattered with blue glacial lakes. Ocean Drive, with its series of scenic overlooks, cleaves to the shore, but 120 miles of hiking trails and fifty miles of graveled carriage paths scale the mountains and

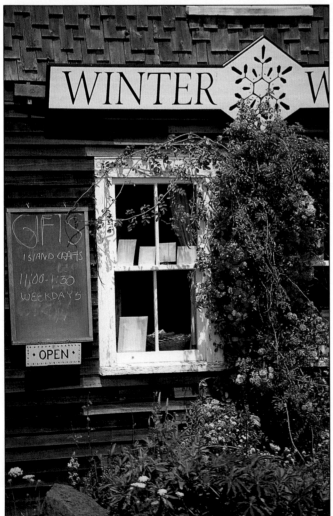

Above: *a whiplash of line highlighted by the evening sun on Rangely Lakes at dusk.*

Left: *a Wonheg Winter Works window on Monhegan Plantation, Monhegan Island.*

Right: *a nature trail in the Seawall area, Acadia National Park, Mount Desert Island.*

crisscross the wooded interior. The resort town of Bar Harbor gave even Newport a run for its money during the flowering of its Gilded Age. More primal in its appeal is Thunder Hole, where the heavy surf crashes into a hollow, compressing the air at the rear to produce fantastic booms and a roar deceptively like rolling thunder. Fortunately, Mount Desert's natural wonders are preserved within the boundaries of Acadia National Park – the only one in New England.

Though much of the population and most of the vacationers stick to the shore, Maine is a good deal more than its coastline. The state's vast interior represents for many the proverbial New England wilderness. In its center sits Mt. Katahdin – northern terminus of the Appalachian Trail – knifing upward a mile out of its plain in magisterial isolation. The

interior has about twenty-five hundred lakes and large ponds, while its rivers and streams number more than five thousand. Indians fished the waters for thousands of years before they were joined by an elite corps of rusticating fly fishermen. The mostly wooded interior also includes Maine's northernmost county, Aroostock, whose flat and now-treeless expanses of "caribou loam" have made it one of the world's premier potato belts, and where school traditionally closes for three weeks in September so even the children can help bring in the multi-billion-pound harvests.

As it was for Thoreau 150 years ago, the city of Bangor is often the point of departure into the interior. Historically, Bangor – some thirty miles up the Penobscot – was the place where the Maine forest and the ocean met. In the rollicking days of the mammoth timber drives, lumberjacks floated logs from upstream to the Bangor mills, where they were shaped into boards, shingles, clapboards, and lath, then dispatched downriver toward distant trading ports. Thoreau first journeyed to Bangor in 1838 in search of a teaching job. Though disappointed in his original quest, he got bitten by the bug to explore Maine's interior. Over the course of two decades, he returned to make three interior journeys, traveling by batteau with Maine rivermen and with Penobscot Indians by birch bark canoe. The separate accounts Thoreau wrote of the voyages were gathered after his death into *The Maine Woods*, which provides the classic descriptions of Maine's inland wilderness.

Thoreau was dismayed by the mills and lumber

Above: *a Wiscasset wreck.*

Left: *Beaver Island on Aziscoos Lake, Lincoln Plantation.*

camps, where the "mission of men . . . seems to be, like so many busy demons, to drive the forest all out of the country, from every solitary beaver-swamp and mountain-side, as soon as possible." And yet, in a few hours' travel toward the interior's "wild and unsettled" stretch, he found himself carried "to the verge of a primitive forest, more interesting, perhaps, on all accounts, than [one] would reach by going a thousand miles westward." It was this primitive country that inspired Thoreau to some of his most stirring and rapturous heights. Coming down Mt. Katahdin, he "most fully realized that this was primeval, untamed, and forever untameable *Nature,* . . . that Earth of which we have heard, made out of Chaos and Old Night, . . . the fresh and natural surface of the planet . . . as it was made for ever and ever. . . . It was Matter, vast, terrific . . . to be inhabited by men nearer of kin to the rocks and to wild animals than we. . . . What is this Titan that has possession of me? Talk of mysteries!"

Spring lays lightly on a farm's lush pasture in North Baldwin.

The Maine interior may be somewhat less mysterious than it was in Thoreau's time. You can drive to Baxter State Park to see Mt. Katahdin, along with spectacular waterfalls, glacial ponds, and huge, pink granite boulders. If you want to stay at one of the many well-equipped campgrounds in the park, you'll probably need advance reservations. But six and a half million acres of northern Maine still remain effectively inaccessible, served only by private roads, and many recesses of the deep forest can only be reached by white-water canoe along the maze of inland waterways. On the streambanks and at pond's edge, it's not unusual to be surprised by the brooding stare of the eastern moose. Through the lake mists, you're likely to hear the shrill, otherworldly cry of the loon. Even toward the close of the twentieth century, the Maine interior endures as a frontier for the senses and spirit.

Above: *a view of Camden Harbor and Penobscot Bay from Mount Battie.*

Left: *colorful rowing boats moored in Bar Harbor on Mount Desert Island.*

Facing page: *Pemaquid Light standing squarely amid the rocks of Pemaquid Point.*

141

Above: *farm buildings blending with the trees in North Baldwin.*

Below: *Perkins Cove Candy shop in Ogunquit village.*

Right: *Georgian Hamilton House, South Berwick.*

Facing page: *a reminder of
yesteryear outside a barn in
Standish, southern Maine.*

Above: *an aerial view of an
immaculate farmhouse and
fields in rural Maine.*

Right: *a blue flag iris and
weathered wood on Great Wass
Island Preserve, off Jonesport.*

145

Wind-sculpted snow in the little village of Phillips, which lies on the Sandy River near the Rangely Lakes region.

Facing page: *apple blossom in the town park frames a tranquil view across Rockport harbor.*

Above: *pulled clear of a spring tide, a rowing boat lies in marsh grass near Freeport, north of Brunswick.*

Right: *cheerful tubs of geraniums grace the harbor wall of Boothbay.*

Maine

Above: *boats moored beside the lobster pound as dusk descends in Owl's Head harbor.*

Left: *the rugged shoreline of Scarborough, its rocks touched by late afternoon light.*

Right: *a morning in fall in the Boothbay Harbor area, one of Maine's best boating centers.*

Above: *a pair of cross-country skiers near Jackson. Cross-country ski trails have been laid out all over the state.*

Left: *the 1906 lion-head fountain, a feature of Seal Harbor, one of the entrances to Acadia National Park.*

Facing page: *Abol Stream in Baxter State Park, a densely forested tract of wilderness in the heart of the state.*

Above: *skis, a scythe, a stepladder and shutters comprise part of a motley collection at a Vermont barn sale.*
Right: *high summer in the countryside outside Reading.*

*V*ermont

Vermont's reputation for maverick independence dates back to an especially contentious colonial history. In 1764, taking broad license with his royal charter, New Hampshire Governor Benning Wentworth started granting towns west of the Connecticut River. New York also laid claim to the area between Connecticut and Lake Champlain. When the King ruled against Wentworth in 1770, New York's Governor George Clark sent his agents to evict the New Hampshire grantees, or make them pay for their land a second time, lining the pockets of New York collectors.

Ethan Allen and his Green Mountain Boys launched the first American offensive of the Revolution, capturing Fort Ticonderoga from the British in 1775, but the vigilante group was actually organized to wage an armed resistance against Clark and his "Yorkers." It was toward the Yorkers that Allen addressed his famous remark, "The gods of the hills are not the gods of the valleys" – which one historian has loosely translated as "come and get me."

Even after the Revolution was over, the Allen Brothers weren't ready to give up their own civil war. In 1777, they organized a stormy, week-long convention in a tavern at Windsor where Vermont was declared an independent republic. Four years later, Allen vowed in a letter to Congress: "I am as resolutely determined to defend the independence of

Above: *the station weathervane at White River Junction.*

Above: *inquisitive cows on a snowy Vermont farm.*

Left: *geese guardians break the calm of an autumn afternoon.*

Right: *downhill skiing on Jay Peak, which is 3,861 feet high.*

Vermont as Congress that of the United States, and rather than fail will retire with the hardy Green Mountain Boys into the desolate caverns of the mountains and wage war with human nature at large." The fight didn't end for plucky Vermont until 1791, when the Green Mountain State was finally admitted as the fourteenth in the union.

The document drafted and signed at the tavern table in Windsor's Old Constitution House was the most radical of its day – prohibiting slavery, granting universal suffrage to males whether or not they owned property, and mandating free public education. Vermont has perpetuated that progressive tradition, in contrast to its conservative neighbor across the Connecticut. During the 1980s, in Burlington, the

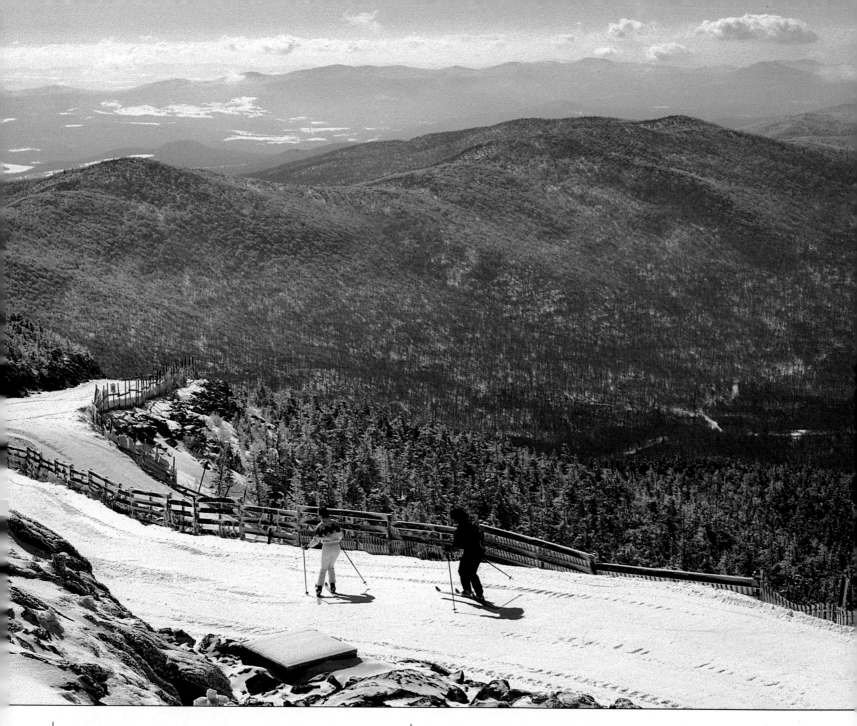

state's only city with a hundred thousand-plus population, Bernard Sanders – a Socialist and a transplanted "flatlander," from Brooklyn no less – served four terms as mayor. Those who would chalk up Sanders's reign to the aberrant influence of Burlington's granola-chomping intellectuals should consider that in 1988, Sanders was barely edged out by Republican Peter Smith in the statewide race for Vermont's U.S. congressional seat, or that the state has had a three-term woman governor in Madeleine Kunin. Kunin is known nationwide for her outspoken views on environmental issues like acid rain, but Vermonters have long been ecologically minded. Among the many distinguished citizens of the shire town of Woodstock, Vermont, was George Perkins Marsh, author of the 1864 *Man and Nature* and America's first environmentalist. Marsh's legacy lives on in the only state in the country with a billboard ban, where newcomers band together with natives to fight shopping malls, condo complexes, and abuses of ski-resort development.

This enlightened culture sets the tone for Montpelier, the country's smallest seat of state government, where the gold Capitol dome topped by a statue of Ceres rises above more recent local landmarks like the vegetarian Horn of the Moon Cafe, whose bulletin board announces classes in Afro-Cuban drumming and dance and demonstrations against U.S. policy in Central America. Montpelier's twin city of Barre presents a different, though no less colorful

Above: *the U.S. Post Office in Grafton, southern Vermont.*

Below: *flamingos and dance wear in a Battleboro store.*

facet of the Vermont heritage. A carved plaque at the city limits identifies Barre as the "Granite Capital of the World"; since the early 1800s, more than a hundred quarrying companies have harvested Barre's granite and marble deposits. After the Central Vermont Railroad ran its tracks to Barre in 1875, the population more than tripled inside of a decade with the influx of skilled stonecutters from Italy, Scotland, and Scandinavia. The granite capital turned as boisterous as any logging camp, but the action wasn't all in the pubs and saloons. The explosive mix of underpaid immigrant workers made the town a hotbed of radical politics and host to international figures like anarchist Emma Goldman, who was arrested there.

The former Socialist meeting hall, doorway graced by a granite hammer and sickle, is now a tomato cannery resting on a quiet side street. But on a rise

Vermont's gilded state capitol, the pride of Montpelier.

above town, the century-old, 350-foot-deep, twenty-acre Rock of Ages quarry still hums, spilling its waterfalls of discarded granite chunks over the hillsides. In the nearby countryside, a quarry abandoned at the turn of the century when workers hit an underground spring makes a deep, cold, and dramatic swimming hole. And in Barre's Hope Cemetery, the art of the immigrant stonecutters is preserved in the monuments they carved for themselves and their families. William and Gwendolyn Halvosa's tomb sports a large double portrait of the couple sitting up beside each other in bed; the elegant, life-sized likeness of Elia Corti was carved as a tribute by his fellow craftsmen after Corti was shot in 1903, while trying to calm a dispute between Socialist and Anarchist stone-cutters.

Northwest of the Barre-Montpelier area, Stowe embodies a side of Vermont more familiar to the state's vacationing visitors. Tiny Stowe village, with its white frame houses and steepled church sends one back to an earlier century, but the drive up the Stowe Mountain Road, lined with restaurants, lodges, and quaintly designed shopping plazas, brings you into the world of the modern ski resort. Among Stowe's four-star inns is the Trapp Family Lodge, opened by the Baroness Maria von Trapp of *Sound of Music* fame, who found the landscape reminiscent of her native Austria.

What draws skiiers to Stowe besides the edelweiss atmosphere is Mt. Mansfield, Vermont's highest peak, equipped not only with the famous downhill runs but also a Nordic ski center, an auto road, a series of hiking trails, a gondola, and a hair-raising twenty-three-hundred-foot Alpine slide. Beyond the mountain

development is the high pass called Smugglers' Notch, with a winding road as steep as many ski trails and closed through the winter. Illegal traffic through the Notch has included cattle for the British Army during the War of 1812, fugitive slaves, and boot-leggers' whiskey. As you navigate the winding passage of the treacherous Notch, it's important to remember that many of Vermont's peaks have escaped Mansfield-style development. The only way to get up the majestic Camel's Hump is to hike, but climbers are rewarded by the summit's Alpine zone and the spectacular vistas, ranging on a clear day from Mt. Washington in the east to the westward expanse of the Champlain valley, the glistening Lake Champlain itself, and on its far shores, New York's Adirondacks.

Camel's Hump's brooding summit aside, the Green Mountains are supposed to be gentler than the Whites, and Vermont's countryside tamer than Maine's wild interior. The state is indeed the fabled haven of rounded hills, tranquil valleys, beautiful hamlets, and family dairy farms the picturebook image would have you expect. From Newfane to Craftsbury Common, West Tunbridge to Warren, the charming country villages are too numerous to name, their secrets too precious to sketch in summary. What you need is a trustworthy map of back roads and a frame of mind that affords the leisure to travel them.

Another helpful guide might be a calendar of special local events. What better time to discover a town than on the morning of the farmers' market or antiques auction, the evening of the grange barbecues or the band concert on the village green? Summer is

Above: *black cane rockers invite repose in Newfane, a southern Vermont town.*

Right: *a covered bridge near Saxon's River in Grafton, one of Vermont's loveliest towns.*

Left: *Shadow lake in the White Mountains at Concord Corner, close to Jackman Mountain.*

traditionally festival season, and Vermont offers everything from hot-air balloon fests to juried fine crafts shows to old-time country fairs, where the attractions still include the perennial favorite, the ox-pull, in which man and beast team up to provide a fascinating display of brute force and character.

Summer isn't the only time to hunt down a festival. On the frozen lake along its unique barrel-buoyed Floating Bridge, the village of Brookfield hosts an annual Ice Harvest, a celebration of the era before refrigeration, when townsfolk used giant handsaws and long-handled tongs to bring out great squares of ice that, packed in sawdust to insulate them, lasted through August.

Perhaps one way to exit gracefully from the maze of back roads is to visit two corners of the state that,

Above: early morning fishing on Lake Champlain.

Right: chess players ensconced in a Vermont store in winter.

in their own way, reflect as much of a contrast as the jump, in Vermont's neighbors to the east, from mountain to coastline. Shelburne, on the shores of Lake Champlain, enjoys a milder climate than much of the state. It is here that the wealthy Webb family sunk its fortune into the creation of the Shelburne Museum, one of the world's finest and most extensive repositories of Americana. Actually, it's hard to think of the Shelburne collections as a museum. Covering everything from period toys to vintage quilts to folk art weathervanes, they're spread over forty-five landscaped acres and contained in thirty-five historic structures, including a stage coach inn, a covered bridge, a lighthouse, the sidewheeler *Ticonderoga*, which cruised Lake Champlain for nearly fifty years, and a huge, horseshoe-shaped barn that houses a hundred antique coaches, sleighs, and carriages.

At another end of the spectrum lies the Northeast Kingdom, Vermont's last frontier, comprising two thousand square miles of the state's three northern counties. Huddled against the Canadian border, Vermont's remote and rustic hinterland – what its local bard, novelist Howard Frank Mosher, has called "Kingdom Come" – is a province of French Canadian loggers and Allen Brothers-style renegades, a land of lakes and near-wilderness where the Prohibition-era shoot-outs between lawmen and rum-runners still reverberate through the woods. It's also the poorest

Facing page: *West Guilford Baptist Church.*

Facing page: *Virginia creeper falls across a shed in Tunbridge.*

Above: *a sparkling fall day in West Burke, northeast Vermont.*

Above: *a rusting car blends with South Strafford leaves.*

part of the state, home to pockets of Appalachian-style rural poverty few tourists see, or fit into their conception of the pristine Vermont countryside.

Vermont is a fitting place to wind up our New England pilgrimage, since for many, it's the state that best mirrors the New England ethos. Vermont is the most rural and least populous of the six states. Vermonters tap the most maples, milk the most cows, and burn the most wood per capita. The folkloric jokes about those crustily reticent Yankees directing lost flatlanders into backwoods oblivion really do have their basis in fact, as travelers discover each year along Vermont's roadsides. What may be astonishing about the state, as this century winds to its close, is how much truth is still preserved in the jokes and the popular images.

The same could be said for the whole of New England. When Vermont folk historian Dorothy Canfield Fisher described her native state more than fifty years ago, she might just as well have been reflecting on the region in general: " Vermont . . . is a piece of the past in the midst of the present and the future." Happily, there are enough of us who love New England, both from here at home and from afar, that there's reason to hope it will stay that way.

Above: *winter light and white water outside the Vermont Guild of Old Time Crafts and Industries, Weston.*

Left: *Grafton cattle grazing on the last of summer's grass before the snows of fall cover the land until spring.*

*Newspaper holders,
Weathersfield Bow, a common
sight along Route 5.*

Above: *moonlight in Vermont; a floodlit steeple in Waites River lends a mystical quality to a midwinter night.*

Left: *silver birches in their spring livery near Post Mills. These trees are destined to turn a muted gold in the fall.*

Above: *wraith-like bands of mist due to clear after the sun has risen in rural Vermont.*

Left: *golden rod brightens a pasture fence at Green River in the extreme south of the state.*

Facing page: *a swing on a maple tree, Hartford. The user is assured a fine view.*

Vermont

Above: *maple syrup sap test bottles in a Franklin window.*

Above: *moonrise over Old First Church in Bennington on a winter's evening.*

Left: *spring water overflows from a strategically placed bucket in Chelsea.*

Left: *trompe l'oeil mural on a Montpelier wall, one of several such murals in the state capital.*

173

Above: *snow in East Orange, a small town that lies southeast of Barre, close to one of the state's public hunting areas.*

Right: *an ornamental street clock in Battleboro, the site of the first permanent settlement in the state.*

Above: *Middlebury, where a pristine Congregational Church dominates the skyline in a town of Victorian-style buildings.*

Right: *a Vermont barn sale, which features items as varied as bottles, books, bathroom scales and a piano stool.*